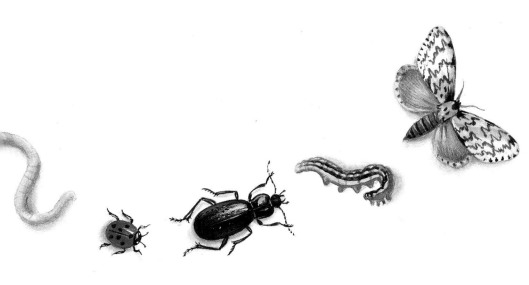

Published by Silver Dolphin Books
5880 Oberlin Avenue, Suite 400
San Diego, CA 92121-9653
1-800-284-3580

Library of Congress Cataloging-in-Publication Data available on request.

ISBN 1-57145-325-3

Conceived and produced by Breslich & Foss Ltd, London

Designed by Roger Daniels
Original text by Caroline Taylor
Printed and bound in Hong Kong

The Secret Garden

ACTIVITY BOOK

**15 Gardening and Nature Projects
Based on the Classic Story**

Illustrated by
GRAHAM RUST

SILVER DOLPHIN

BOOKS

Contents

Introduction

Perhaps you, like Mary in *The Secret Garden*, have been given "a bit of earth" to grow things in. If you have, this book will help you with ideas about what to grow, and how to go about it. It also reminds you how Dickon made friends with birds and animals, and shows you how to encourage them to share your secret garden.

Planning Your Secret Garden

"Might I," quavered Mary, "might I have a bit of earth?"
Mr. Craven looked quite startled. "Earth!" he repeated. "What do you mean?"
"To plant seeds in—to make things grow—to see them come alive."

∽

Mary and Dickon had high walls around their secret garden, and the only way in was through a door hidden by a curtain of ivy. (The robin showed Mary the key.) But your garden will feel quite secret if it is screened from your house behind a bit of something—a bush, a tree, a garden shed, or even some low fencing.

It doesn't need to be a big patch, but it does need to be sunny if you are to grow flowers and vegetables. You can always make a shady spot later. So, if you are being offered somewhere to make a garden, do make sure that the grown-ups understand that.

If your garden is big enough, it helps to divide it up. You could grow flowers in one section, vegetables in another, wildflowers for butterflies in a third, and keep a rabbit hutch in a fourth. Perhaps you could persuade someone to make narrow paths between the sections. They do not need to be wide enough for you or Mary to skip down, but they will stop you from trampling the earth when you are gardening or picking vegetables. They could be steppingstones, half-size concrete paving stones, bricks, or old boards. Perhaps you could also persuade someone to make a fence around your garden.

Plots and plans

Make a list of the things you would like to include in your garden. (You may not get them all!) Then draw some plans to show how it could be laid out. You need to turn the soil over with a garden fork, get all the weeds out with your trowel, and rake it smooth before you start making paths, planting, or sowing seeds. If you can get hold of some compost, mix this into the earth to help your plants to grow. Compost is a rich food that plants love. If you are lucky, there will be worms in your patch of earth. Be careful not to harm the worms when you are digging.

Did you know?

Worms help gardeners by bringing air and plant food down into the soil. You can see how worms work if you put alternate layers of damp soil and sand in a jar, with rotting leaves at the top, and add a couple of worms. Tie dark paper round the jar, punch some holes in the lid, and leave the jar in a cool place. When you remove the paper, what do you find?

"There's naught as nice as the smell o' good clean earth, except th' smell o' fresh growing things when th' rain falls on 'em," said Dickon.

Essential Garden Tools

"I've got th' garden tools. There's a little spade an' rake an' a fork an' hoe. Eh! they're good 'uns. There's a trowel, too."

⤎⤏

Dickon bought garden tools for Mary from the shop in the village on the moors. They all have their special purposes, but your trowel will do most jobs once the soil is prepared. You can weed with it, dig holes with it, plant with it.

Spades are used for heavy digging and for lifting large plants; forks for breaking up clods of earth and for digging gently round plants; rakes are for smoothing the surface before sowing grass seed or vegetables; and hoes are for weeding out weeds

between rows of vegetables and in other places that you cannot easily reach.

You will also need a watering can with a sprinkler at the end (which is much better for plants than a fierce hose), and some pots to grow plants in. And if you grow roses, you will need some thick gloves to protect you from the thorns.

It is important to keep tools clean and dry when you are not using them. A clutter of muddy tools in a corner is a gloomy sight. Make sure you wipe or wash the dirt off your trowel before you put it away, and oil the handle occasionally to keep the wood supple and comfortable to hold. A row of clean garden tools hung on nails in a shed or in the garage looks nice and will make you want to use them.

"I wish—I wish I had a little spade," said Mary.

Watching and Collecting Insects

Also you could make the acquaintance of strange busy insect things running about on various unknown but evidently serious errands, sometimes carrying tiny scraps of straw or feather or food, or climbing blades of grass as if they were trees from whose tops one could look out and explore the country.

❧

Have you ever lain quite still on your stomach in a field, or even in the garden, and waited quietly? After a short while, you will hear all kinds of strange little rustlings and you will see insects that you did not know were there. They "froze" when they heard you coming, and many of them (like grasshoppers and crickets) have excellent camouflage, but because you are still and quiet, they stop being frightened and start their busy lives again.

You can also find insects by turning over stones, poking about in old leaves, or gently removing old bark from a rotten log. (Remember to replace whatever you remove; if insects from damp places dry out, they will die.)

To turn yourself into a scientific discoverer, like Colin in *The Secret Garden*, you will need some books on insects from the library, a notebook, and a magnifying bug box. Look closely, then draw or note down what you see. You could start with feeding habits. You may be able to watch a butterfly pollinating a flower as it pauses to drink the nectar; a ladybug feasting on aphids on a rose; moths attracted at dusk by pale flowers that glow in the dark; swallows swooping low over water to catch insects in their beaks; flies consuming a moldy fruit; a column of ants taking food back to "camp"; or greedy caterpillars eating the leaves of flowers in your wildflower garden.

Close-up on wildlife

🦟 Ants follow a scent line. Try diverting them by gently rubbing away a few inches of the route they are following, and see what happens.

🦟 Sink a can in your garden one night (it's cooler and damper then), with the top at the level of the soil, and prop up a cover to keep off the rain. Put a small piece of fruit in the bottom as bait and use a magnifying glass, or the lid from a bug box next morning to examine what you find.

🦟 Make a list of which plants attract most insects, and note what color the plants are.

🦟 Catch insects, so that you can observe them, in a bug box lined with paper or moss. When you have finished, always take the insects back to where you found them. Ladybugs should be kept in a large, clear plastic box so that they can fly. Cut a rose shoot covered in aphids and stand it in a jar of water in a box. You can then watch the ladybugs feed on the aphids.

Did you know?

Insects have six legs—so a spider is not an insect.

Most insects have wings at one point in their lives—though a flea does not.

Insects are invertebrates—they don't have a backbone.

Insects are an essential part of the chain of life. It is easy to appreciate insects that are useful to humans, like butterflies and moths (which pollinate flowers), bees (which make honey), and ladybugs (which eat the aphids that damage plants). But even pests, like flies (which spread disease) and weevils and locusts (which eat crops), provide food for birds, bats, and reptiles, while beetles eat dead plants and animals and turn then back into earth.

They drew the chair under the plum-tree, which was snow-white with blossoms and musical with bees.

Planting a Spring Garden

She thought she saw something sticking out of the black earth—some sharp little pale green points.

"Yes, they are tiny growing things and they might be crocuses or snowdrops or daffodils," she whispered.

O ne of the most exciting things in the garden is when you see the earth beginning to come to life again after the winter. Those "sharp little pale green points" suddenly turn into crocuses, sweet-scented hyacinths, and tulips with their brilliant petals.

Later in the spring, your garden could be yellow with daffodils or narcissi. Choose the shorter ones (tall ones look top-heavy in a small space) like "February Gold" or "Peeping Tom." All daffodils look best grown in grass. Tulips look lovely in grass, in beds, or in pots, and there are lots of colors to choose from. You can order bulbs from a catalog, or buy them from a garden center.

Planting action

Most spring bulbs should be planted in the autumn. Use your trowel and plant them at least twice as deep as the height of the bulb. If you live in a very cold climate, you could grow snowdrops. Snowdrop bulbs should not be allowed to dry out, but should be planted just after flowering, when they are still "green." Whenever you plant, use markers to remind you where the bulbs are, and write their names on stickers.

"Th' very little ones are snowdrops and crocuses an' th' big ones are narcissus and jonquils an' daffydowndillys," said Martha. "Eh! they are nice. Dickon's got a whole lot of 'em planted in our bit o' garden."

Watching Birds

When she stood still she saw a bird with a bright red breast sitting on the topmost branches, and suddenly he burst into his winter song.

"He's a robin redbreast," said Ben Weatherstaff, "and they're th' friendliest, curiousest birds alive."

⸜⸝

If you are busy in your garden in winter, you may notice a robin with its red breast hopping about near you, curious to see what you are doing, and ready to gobble up any worms that you may dig up. Other garden birds are shyer, but you may spot speckled thrushes, tiny darting wrens, or busy little chickadees.

If your garden has plenty of safe, secret places—in thick shrubs and climbers, in the branches of trees, in holes in a tree trunk, or in a bird box—it may contain nests. Sit quietly by a window, or in a corner of the garden in spring. When you see birds carrying nesting materials in their beaks—twigs, moss, bits and pieces—watch where they take them. If you discover a nest, note how many eggs there are and what they look like: their color, size, shape, and whether they are speckled or plain. Don't touch them, or frighten the adults. Check in a book which birds the eggs belong to.

In the spring, you can watch the birds taking worms, beetles, or insects back to their clamoring babies. Later still, you may be able to watch the babies learning to fly.

A good way of observing birds is to feed them in the winter, when they will be short of food and water. You will attract a wide range of birds if you do this, but once you start feeding them you must continue; they may starve if you stop. Birds will eat most kitchen scraps—fruit, stale cookies, bread, cheese, potatoes, rice. Make sure the birds also have water to drink and bathe in.

Making a bird cake

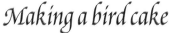

Melt some fat from a roast and stir in wild
bird seed, cake and bread crumbs, nuts, and
some chopped bacon. Pour the mixture
into a round bowl and let it harden. Ease it
from the bowl, and make a hole through the
center with a knitting needle. Thread 2 ft. (60 cm) of
string through the hole, and tie a good big knot at the
bottom. Hang your bird cake from a high branch.

Close-up on birds

Birds fly and move in very characteristic ways.
Some, like robins, hop about on the ground or on
low branches. Others, like swallows, swifts, and
flycatchers fly fast and high. Hawks hover; nuthatches
run up (but not down) the trunks of trees. Why do you
think birds move so differently? Could it be partly to do
with the food they eat?

Look at birds' feathers or "plumage." Males

and females are different, and their plumage often changes from winter to summer as well. Keep a notebook, and write down anything you notice about the birds in your garden. Then check a reference book and see if you can name the birds that you saw.

Did you know?

You can talk to birds, especially robins. Try whistling quietly like Ben Weatherstaff, or imitating the birds' own song. See how they respond. Try this in the winter; the birds will be busy in the spring.

Some birds migrate thousands of miles. If you live in a colder climate, watch how birds gather in the autumn before they set off for a warmer place. And keep an eye out for "strangers" at your bird table in winter.

"I'll call the robin up," Dickon said, "and give him th' rind o' th' bacon to peck at. They likes a bit o' fat wonderful."

Keeping your Garden Tidy

She knelt down and dug and weeded out the weeds and grass until she made nice little clear places around them.

∞

Weeding is one of those comfortable things to do when the sun is beginning to warm your back in the spring, and spring is the time when you can get weeds out most easily. Use your trowel for this, but take care not to damage other plants as well. Some weeds are easier to pull out with your fingers.

Weeds are wild plants that appear where you do not want them. There are annual ones that seed themselves from year to year, and perennial ones that stay around all the time until you dig them out. Weeds gobble up the goodness in the soil, and can even choke precious garden plants. Mary saw that the plants in the Secret Garden needed to "breathe." Many weeds, like daisies, dandelions, and buttercups, have pretty flowers, but they will all, in one way or another, try to take over your garden. Weed them out, and transfer the pretty ones to your wildflower patch.

Grasses are one of the most invasive weeds, seeding as well as running underground. Dandelions are probably the hardest to get out—you must work hard to dig the whole long taproot out; if you leave a bit, it will grow again. But whatever they are, try to get the weeds out before they have a chance to seed themselves again.

Did you know?

You should always put weeds in the trash can, or in the incinerator. If you put them in the compost bin their seeds will probably germinate with new vigor next year.

"Why, I thought tha' didn't know nothin' about gardenin'," Dickon exclaimed. "A gardener couldn't have told thee better."

Watching Animals

A boy was sitting under a tree, and on the trunk of the tree a brown squirrel was clinging and watching him, and from behind a bush nearby a cock pheasant was delicately stretching his neck to peep out, and quite near him were two rabbits sitting up and sniffing with tremulous noses.

∞

Most wild animals are shy of humans. If you live in the country you will know that you must move quietly if you are not to frighten them away. If you live in a town, you will have seen squirrels running along walls and fences and leaping up into the trees. You may have seen little mice nipping round corners of the garden, or even larger animals nosing about.

Even if you haven't seen the wild animals themselves—and many of them hole up during the day and only emerge at dusk—you may have seen signs that they are nearby. You can see their tracks in the snow: the long feet of a rabbit; the paw marks of a possum or a raccoon; or the tiny claw marks of mice. An animal's droppings will often tell you that they are there (and sometimes what they have eaten): look out for rabbits' droppings, or an owl's pellets.

You may notice where squirrels have disturbed the ground under the trees—burying or digging up nuts. You may see fallen fruit with tell-tale gnaw marks of a rodent with sharp front teeth. You will know the marks of a horse's shod hoof in soft ground but you may have to look closely to see the marks left by lighter animals. You may see teeth marks on a tree where squirrels have nibbled the sappy bark.

Keeping domestic animals

Domestic animals are responsive and will enjoy your company. You can also learn a lot about the way animals behave from keeping one. Rabbits or guinea pigs can be kept in a cage in your garden—though they will need to come in to a sheltered place if the weather turns cold. Hamsters and white mice should be kept indoors. All animals need plenty of fresh water, the right food, and warm, dry bedding. Cages must be cleaned out regularly so that they don't become smelly.

Guinea pigs, which come from South America, make easy pets and can also be kept outside. They are less likely than rabbits to burrow their way out of a run on the grass. Hamsters are more delicate and must be kept warm and dry and away from draughts. They should be kept in a large cage that includes a separate sleeping shed. Hamsters love to exercise on special climbing frames and treadmills that you can buy for them.

In spite of their fierce red eyes, white mice are friendly little creatures. Because they need only a small cage they can be moved from place to place more easily than other pets. They reproduce frequently and have many babies.

Did you know?

🐌 Some wild animals, like foxes, squirrels, and raccoons, have learned to live in towns—and even prefer it.

🐌 Dusk and the very early morning are the best times for watching wild animals.

🐌 Wild animals are fun to watch, but never approach them. They can bite!

"I got up slow," Dickon explained, "because if tha' makes a quick move it startles `em. A body `as to move gentle and speak low when wild things is about."

Planning a Vegetable Garden

Dickon worked in his vegetable garden, planting or tending potatoes and cabbages, turnips and carrots and herbs for his mother.

❧

The important thing about a vegetable plot is that you grow things that you like to eat (though the grown-ups might be glad of some herbs as well). So what do you like? Zucchini, lettuces, beans, tomatoes, squashes, pumpkins, cucumbers, eggplant, sweet peppers?

Draw up a list (don't be too ambitious!), and ask the grown-ups what things will or won't grow well in your area. Then find a gardening book that will tell you when to sow the seeds and how to grow your chosen vegetables. But begin thinking about your vegetable plot early in the year: some seeds will need sowing in the autumn and some must be started off in pots on the windowsill, before you can transplant the seedlings into the garden.

Your vegetable plot

Vegetables look nicest if you grow them in blocks—squares or rectangles or triangles of the same plant—though they also look good in neat rows. You will need narrow pathways between the different vegetables so that you can reach your plants. Vegetables also look nice mixed in with flowers and herbs: marigolds, poppies, pansies, catmint for your cats, parsley or flowery chives, or an edging of little alpine strawberries. Later in the year, you could grow brightly colored, peppery nasturtiums, which you can also use in salads. That way you don't notice the gaps when you pick the vegetables.

If you are short of space in your plot, you could get climbing varieties of beans, peas, or squashes, and grow them up a frame of sticks. Runner beans come with white or red flowers, and you could grow both kinds together. You could grow lovely scented sweet peas at the same time.

Vegetables will feed you. In return, you must give them the conditions they like and plenty of nourishment so that they grow well. There are two main ways of growing vegetables. You can either dig the soil well in the autumn, to bury any weeds and aerate the soil, or you can have a "lazy bed" which you never dig at all, but on which you pile compost every year. The lazy system is useful for raised beds or for growing vegetables in containers, but you do have to work hard to keep down the weeds. If you follow the digging method, you can spread compost on the surface of the soil and the worms will take it down.

Sowing vegetable seeds

It's best to sow your vegetable seeds in a seed bed in a corner; then, because plants germinate at different speeds, you can plant them out in their permanent positions when they are big enough. You should water the plot before sowing or planting out, and give your little plants plenty of water as they grow—do it gently with a watering can so that you don't wash them away. Keep them well weeded so that they don't have to compete for nourishment. Pick your peas, beans, and zucchini as soon as they are ready so that the plant will keep on producing more; and remember that all vegetables taste best when they are young.

Did you know?

You should move your crops from year to year. Different types of vegetables take different nutrients from the soil, and the soil may get tired if you always grow the same vegetable in the same place.

Dickon had bought penny packages of flower seeds now and then and sown bright sweet-scented things among gooseberry bushes and even cabbages.

Planning a Picnic

"I'll tell thee what, lad," Mrs. Sowerby said to Dickon. "When tha' goes to 'em in th' morning's tha' shall take a pail o' good new milk an' I'll bake 'em a crusty cottage loaf or some buns wi' currants in 'em, same as you children like."

❧

Picnics can be anything from grand occasions with hampers of prepared food and drink, to a barbecue, or a sandwich, and a bottle of lemonade in a knapsack. But everything tastes different in the open air, and if there are no grown-ups around, so much the better.

Half the fun is preparing your picnic. So, decide what you want to eat and get it ready in the kitchen at home. Don't forget to include something to drink.

Sit on the grass in your garden, or take a picnic blanket, or set up a tent. And if a grown-up visits you, make sure to make him or her welcome, as Dickon and Mary made Mrs. Sowerby welcome in the Secret Garden.

Making your own picnic lemonade

Remove the rind from four lemons and two
oranges with a peeler. Place the rind and
twelve tablespoons of sugar in a big jug. Ask
a grown-up to boil two pints of water, and pour it over
the rind. Squeeze the fruit, and add the juice to the jug.
Give the mixture a good stir, and leave to cool. Strain the
lemonade through a sieve, and bottle it. Taste the
lemonade before you take it along on your picnic: you
may want to dilute it a little, or add sugar.

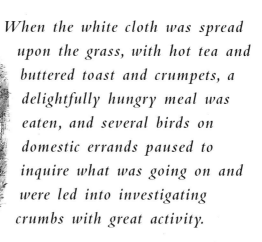

*When the white cloth was spread
upon the grass, with hot tea and
buttered toast and crumpets, a
delightfully hungry meal was
eaten, and several birds on
domestic errands paused to
inquire what was going on and
were led into investigating
crumbs with great activity.*

Growing Roses in Your Garden

"If you wanted to make a flower-garden,"
persisted Mary, "what would you plant?"
"Bulbs an' sweet-smellin' things—but
mostly roses," Ben Weatherstaff replied.

∽

There are so many roses that you could grow! And so many colors and scents. There are climbing roses that will clamber up walls and over shed roofs; there are big, beautiful, scented "old-fashioned" bush roses that mostly flower for a few weeks in June or July—though some, like the Rugosa roses, go on flowering throughout the summer and have wonderful fruit or "hips" in autumn; there are "standard" roses on tall stems; there are smaller "patio" roses that go on flowering all summer and may be the best size for your garden; and there are tiny miniature roses that are usually best grown in a pot.

What fun you will have choosing!

Look at catalogs, books on roses, and at roses in other people's gardens. Or tell someone at your local garden center how big your garden is, and ask for suggestions. Roses usually look better grown in with other flowers so that you don't see their dreary legs.

How to plant a rose

It's easiest to plant a rose that has been grown in a container. Choose a rose that looks sturdy, shiny, and healthy: reject the spindly, sickly ones, and ones with dead brown ends to the shoots. When you are ready to plant, soak the container in a bucket of water until it stops bubbling, then leave it to drain while you dig a hole with a spade. Make the hole wider and deeper than the container, and lay some good rotted compost at the bottom. Put on a good thick pair of gloves. Turn the container upside down, holding the rose stem between the fingers of one hand, and gently tap the plant and the

soil out over the hole you have dug. Wriggle the fingers
of the other hand among the roots to loosen them a bit,

and lower the plant and its soil into the hole.
Carefully fill in around the roots with the
soil you have dug out of the hole, then press
down firmly around the plant. Water the roots
well with your watering can, and keep the plant
watered regularly until it has thoroughly settled in.

Caring for roses

Roses need feeding with a "mulch" of compost in the
spring, and roses that flower all summer will need a
spray-on food that encourages flowering. Ask for help at
your garden center. If roses are healthy and well fed they
should manage without the need to spray against disease.

It is important to deadhead roses, especially the ones
that flower all summer, so that they continue flowering.
Nip the old flowers off, and ask a grown-up to help you
cut the shoot back to just above where you can see
another bud close to the main stem.

It's not essential to prune roses—Mary found roses still alive after ten years—but they will flower better if you do prune them, and they will certainly have a better shape. Perhaps you could ask a grown-up to do this with you.

Did you know?

The swellings on the stems of roses will turn into new shoots.

Leaf buds are the thinner pointed ones, and flower buds are fatter.

There are many different kinds of roses. China roses, Alba roses, Bourbon roses, Damask roses, Moss roses, Tea roses and so on.

And the roses—the roses! Rising out of the grass, tangled round the sun-dial, wreathing the tree-trunks and hanging from their branches, climbing up the walls and spreading over them with long garlands falling in cascades.

Planting a Flower Garden

"There's a lot o' mignonette an' poppies,"
Dickon said. "Mignonette's the sweetest
smellin' thing as grows an' it'll grow
wherever you cast it, same as poppies will.
Them as'll come up an' bloom if you just
whistle to 'em, them's the nicest of all."

With a little planning, you can have flowers
blooming in your garden all summer long. Some
garden flowers are "perennials," which means they come
up year after year; some are "annuals," which germinate,
flower, and die the same year, and must grow from seed
again the next year; some are "biennials," which means
that the foliage starts growing one year, but the plants
only flower the second year; and many are "volunteers,"
which seed themselves.

Look through seed catalogs and at packets of seed
and decide what you want to grow. Mary and
Dickon loved snapdragons, hollyhocks,

columbines, larkspur, pinks, candytuft, marigolds, mignonette, love-in-a-mist, forget-me-nots, poppies, and Canterbury bells. Always buy fresh seed as old seeds deteriorate. The packets will have instructions on sowing and caring for your plants, and will tell you whether they like sun or shade.

Sowing seeds

You can sow hardy annuals straight into the soil where you want them to grow, and you can do this as soon as the soil has warmed up a bit in the spring. Then go on sowing more seed every two weeks or so, so that you have flowers all summer.

First rake the soil in one direction until there are no big lumps. Don't add compost because rich soil encourages flowering plants to produce leaves and not flowers. Then mark out the area where you want these flowers to grow, and scatter your seed thinly over the soil. Rake the soil over the seeds from the opposite

direction and water very gently with a watering can. Write the names of the flowers on your stickers, and place the markers in your flower patch.

Planting seedlings

When you buy little plants, choose sturdy, bushy ones with fat buds. Water the plants in their pots, and leave them to drain. Dig a hole in the raked ground with your trowel, making it large enough for the root ball of the plant. Tip the container up, supporting the plant with a finger on either side of the stem, tap the container and slide the plant into the hole with its soil intact. Firm the soil carefully around the plants, fork the earth a bit between them, and water them in gently.

Caring for your plants

Keep your flowers well watered throughout the summer, and deadhead them whenever you see the flowers are past their best. Snap the flowers off between your finger and thumb. This will make the plants go on producing flowers. Once they have been allowed to go to seed they will feel they have done their job and will give up flowering.

Most annuals will have come to the end of their life by the autumn, and should be raked out and burnt or thrown away. Over the winter you can plan your flower garden for the following year.

Did you know?

You can save seeds from your plants to use again next year. Pick the seedheads or pods in the late summer (try nasturtiums and sweet peas, for example) before they go quite brown and crisp. Let them dry on a sheet of kitchen paper on a tray, and when they are dry enough for the seeds to be released, shake the seeds into an envelope, name it, and store it in a dry place.

The seeds Dickon and Mary had planted grew as if fairies tended them. Satiny poppies of all tints danced in the breeze by the score.

Growing Wildflowers

The low wall at Dickon's cottage was one of the prettiest things in Yorkshire because he had tucked foxgloves and ferns and rockcress and hedgerow flowers into every crevice.

❧

There is something very special about wildflowers—which are the ancestors of all garden flowers. It is thrilling when you see for the first time flowers growing freely in the countryside that you only know in twos and threes in the garden.

If you go to different parts of the country and look about you, you will notice how the wild plant life varies. Plant species evolve to meet the different conditions in which they find themselves. Some flourish in one kind of soil, some in another. Some will survive arctic temperatures at high altitudes; others are tender and will not survive frost at all. Some need hot dry conditions, while others like their feet in water. Some are woodland plants, and others grow best in open, sunny grassland. So before you start planning your wildflower garden you must decide what kind of conditions you can provide for your plants, and discover what kind of wildflowers grow naturally in your area. Wildflowers also bring birds and insects, and especially butterflies, to your garden.

Never pick wildflowers or dig them up. Even when there seems to be an abundance, they can quickly be lost if they are not able to seed and regenerate themselves.

Did you know?

Many wild plants are used in medicine.

Digitalis is the botanic name for foxglove, and digitalis is used to help sufferers from heart disease; quinine, which prevents malaria, is made from the bark of the cinchona tree, and there are many others.

"I wouldn't want to make it look like a gardener's garden, all clipped and spick an' span, would you?" Dickon said. "It's nicer with things running wild."